GRADE 1 READING ACTIVITIES

Fun-filled Activities

An imprint of Om Books International

At the Zoo!

Look at the cover of this book. Then circle the words and pictures you predict will be in this book.

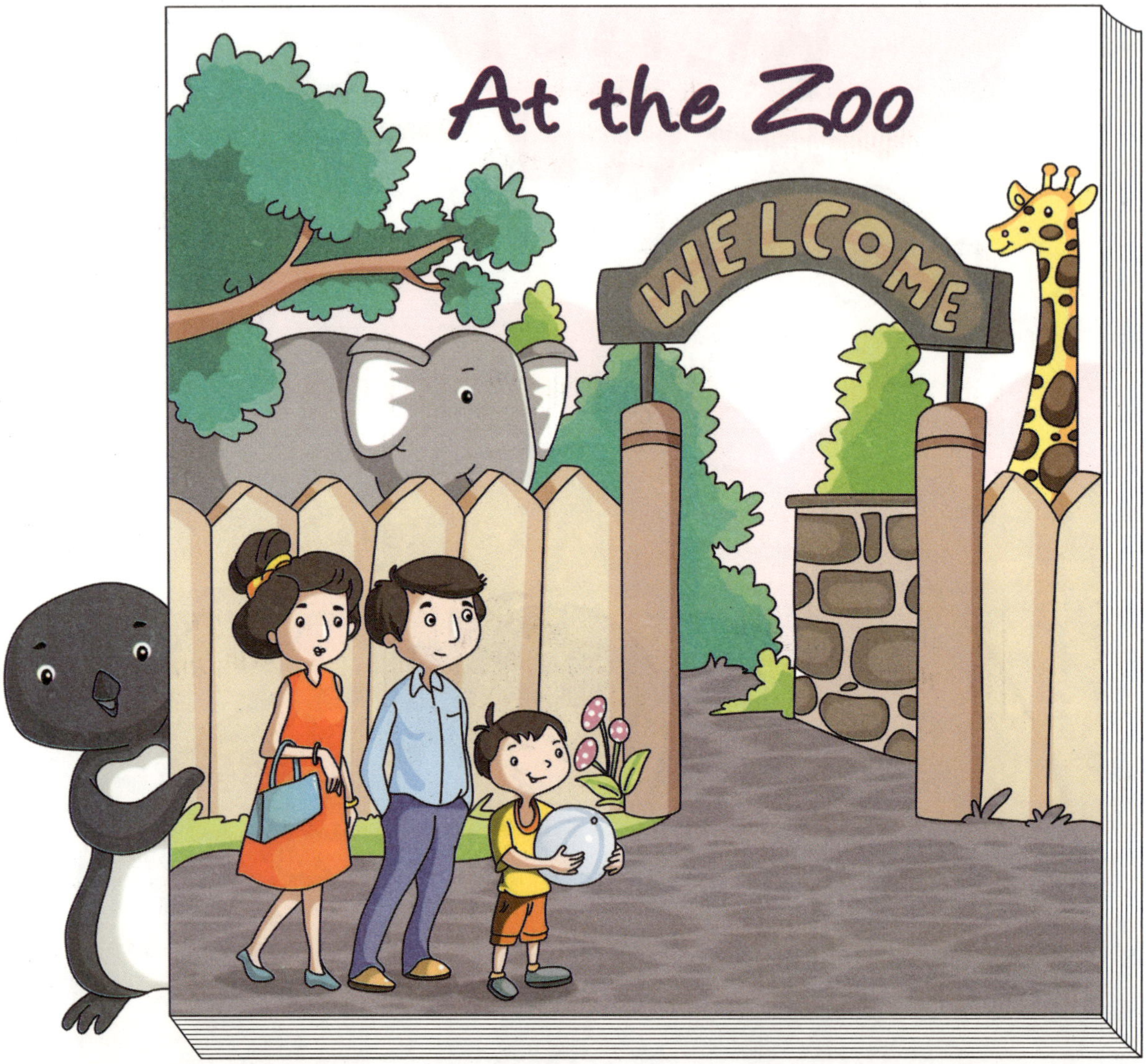

boat

dog

butterfly

elephant

snake

tiger

kite

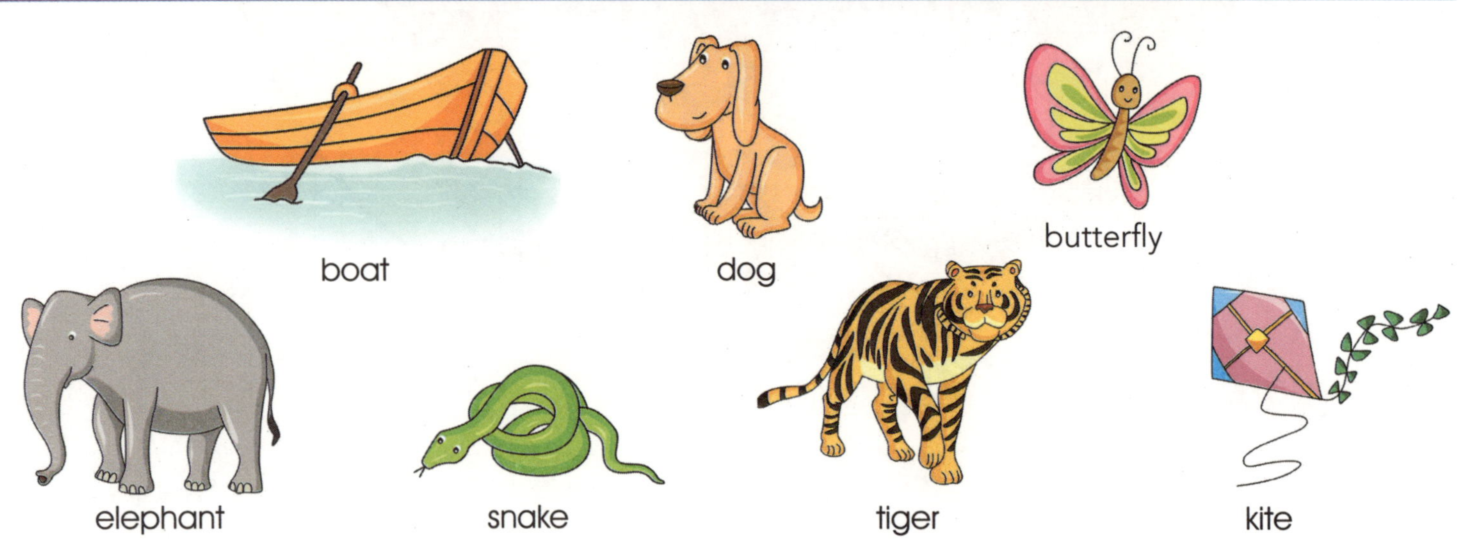

Snack time!

Look at the snack pack.

Take a Break!

Write the name of your favourite snack.

Answer these questions.

1. What is the name of the snack?

2. How much does the snack pack cost?

3. What is free with the pack?

4. How many grams does the pack weigh?

Fish Show!

Circle the right answers.

1. What is the poster about?

   dog show fish show car show

2. When is the show starting?

   June 15 June 10 June 12

3. What is the entry fee for the show?

   $2 $5 $0

4. What are the timings for the show?

   10:00 am-5:00 pm 9:00 am-6:00 pm 6:00 pm-9:00 pm

Wings, Magic and Games too!

Look at the birthday invitation card.

Circle the correct answer

1. Whose birthday is it?

   Alice Melissa Jack

2. How old is Alice?

   four years three years five years

3. When is Alice's birthday?

   January 19 March 19 June 15

4. Where is the birthday to be celebrated?

   Farmland Joy Circus Hotel Blossoms

Take a Break!

What time will Alice's birthday party start? Draw hands on the clock.

Be Safe

Look at a board in the City Zoo.

Tick (✓) the sentence that is right.

1. You should stand on zoo fences. ☐
2. You can feed the animals. ☐
3. Climb over the fence and lean to see the animals. ☐
4. Animals may fall sick by eating your food. ☐
5. Do not tease animals. ☐

Clues about Birds

Read these clues about birds and number them. Then colour them.

1. The yellow bird sleeps in the nest.
2. The blue bird is peeping down.
3. The pink bird flies above the nest.
4. The orange bird is next to the green bird.
5. The green bird winks.

What's the Title?

Circle the words that are shown in the above picture.

jars	boy	bag	pot
stirrer	stool	milk can	sugar
mouse	spoon	napkins	bowl

Your turn!

Which one will you select as the best title for the picture?

1. Cooking with Sam
2. The Cooking Attack
3. It is fun

What Does the Picture Say?

Look at the pictures. Circle the best title from among the given options.

- Benny's basket
- Benny goes on a ride

- Benny with a helmet
- Benny's house

- Sunset time
- Pogo is sad

- Off to sleep
- The Happy Pogo

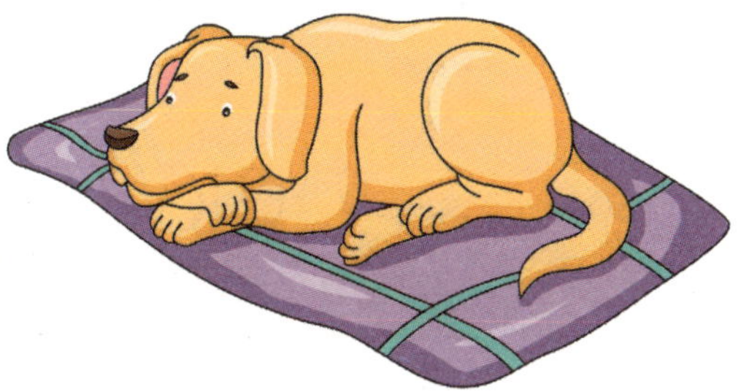

- Let's sing!
- High to fly

- Rock and Roll
- Up and twist

Twist your tongue

Thirty thirsty sailors, sipping pop in pint pots
at a seaside shop
And shaking sandy seashells
on saucy seagulls!

My Own Title!

Look at the pictures. Can you write an interesting title for them?

Make a guess!

I am very thin and small
I have one eye - and that is all!
I am useful to mum
She looks for me when
a stitch is undone!
Who am I?

Mama Duck and Little Duck

Look at the pictures and put a tick (✓) for the correct sentence.

1. Little Duck and Mama Duck walk along the road.

   Little Duck walks along the side of the road.

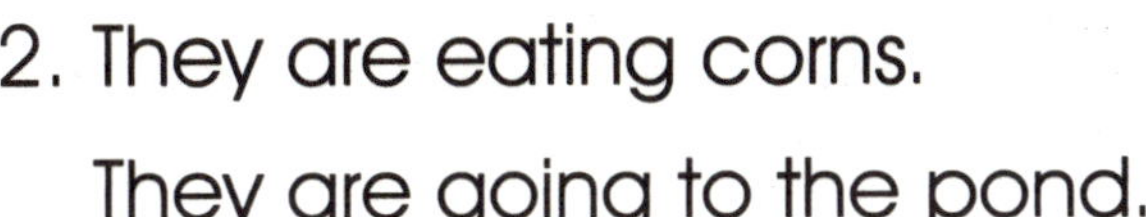

2. They are eating corns.

   They are going to the pond.

3. Little Duck and Mama Duck sit by the pond.

   Little Duck and Mama Duck walk to the field.

4. Mama Duck teaches Little Duck to swim.

   Mama Duck teaches Little Duck to cook.

5. Little Duck swims with Mama Duck every day.

   Little Duck swims by herself now.

Sandy's Tent

Read the sentences. Draw a ◯ around the correct picture.

1. It was raining.

2. Sandy is sad to be at home.

3. Mama built a tent for her to play.

4. Sandy smiled and played.

Maria on a Trip!

Look at the pictures.

Read these sentences and number them according to the pictures. Write 1, 2, 3, 4 and 5.

- [ ] They came back home after a lot of fun.
- [ ] Maria's family went on a trip.
- [ ] They had 3 bags to carry.
- [ ] They also rode on a boat.
- [ ] Maria and her parents went to the beach.

Lucy's Dog

Read the sentences. Number the pictures then.

1. Lucy has a pet dog. She calls it Pog.
2. Pog likes to play fetch with Lucy.
3. Lucy throws a saucer.
4. Pog runs to get the saucer.
5. Pog gives it to Lucy and plays again.

Candy Floss to Eat

Read the words in the picture and write them in correct group.

To eat	To play with	To ride on

Making Lemonade

Read how to make lemonade.

You need: some lemons, sugar, cold water, ice
1. Squeeze some lemons to make lemon juice.
2. Pour the lemon juice into a pitcher and add in some cold water.
3. Add sugar.
4. Stir and put ice.
5. Drink!

Number the pictures 1, 2, 3 and 4 to show the correct order.

A Dog-ear Bookmark

To make a dog-ear bookmark, you need:

a plain envelope, scissors, crayons, ice cream stick and glue

Read the steps to make the bookmark.

Steps:

1. Cut the corner off the edge of an envelope.
2. Draw two eyes and a nose to make the dog's face on the cut-off corner.
3. Now draw 2 half circles under the nose to make the mouth.
4. Draw two droopy ears on the sides.
5. Colour the ears.

Now write 1, 2, 3, 4 and 5 under the pictures to match them with the steps.

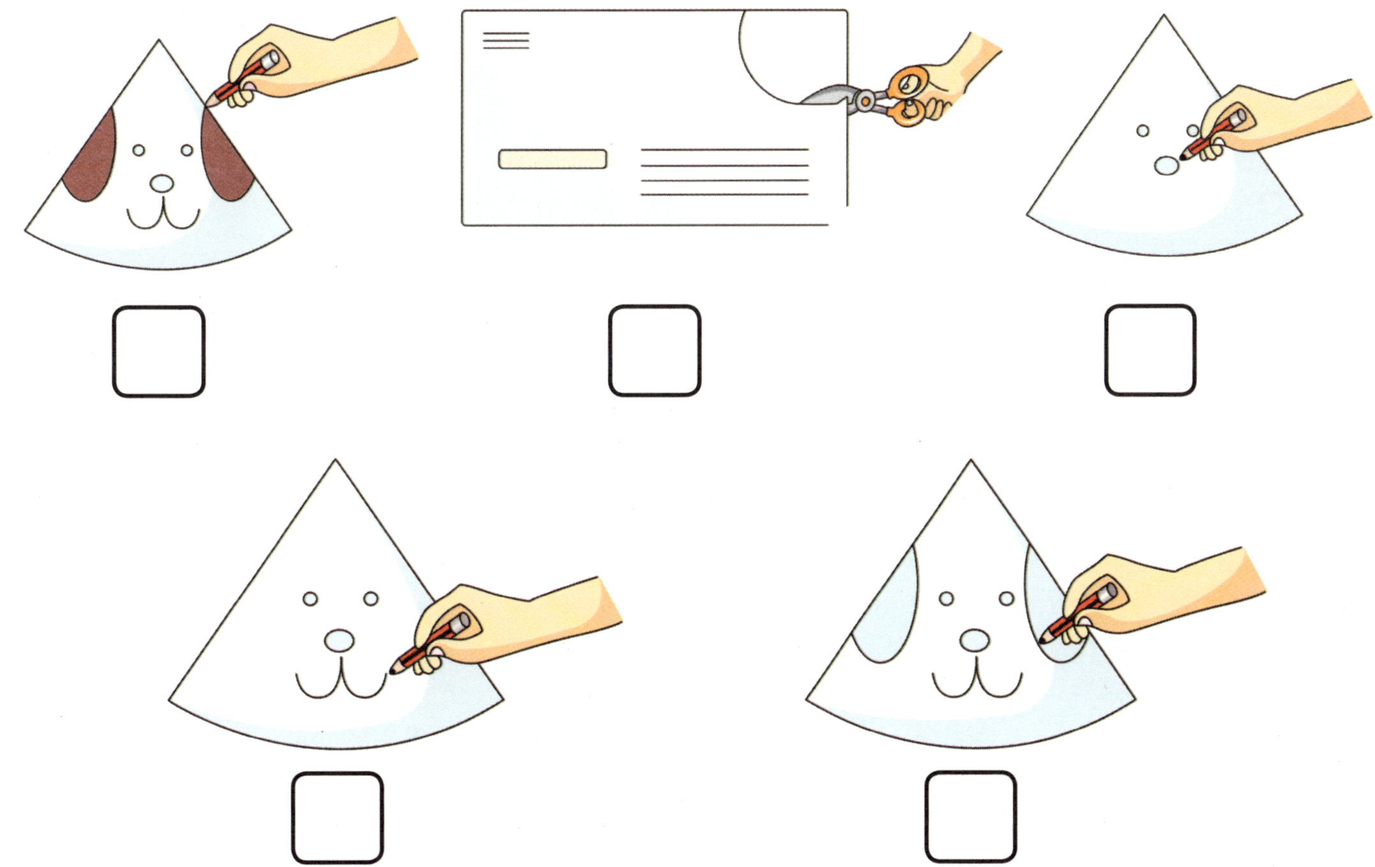

Growing a Plant

Look at the pictures to grow a plant.

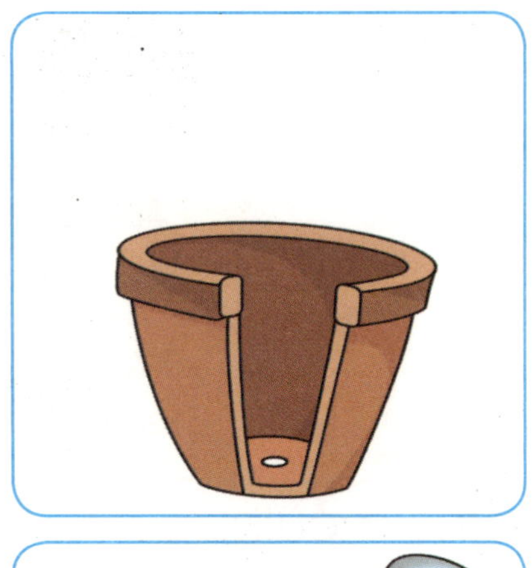

Complete the sentences.

1. Get a ______________.

2. Fill the pot with soil and plant a ______________.

3. Cover with a thin layer of ______________.

4. Add some ______________.

5. Put your pot in ______________ and wait for 1-2 days.

6. Slowly, the ______________ grows.

Five Funny Balloons

Read the poem. Then on each balloon, write the name of the child to which it belongs.

John's pink balloon into the sky
Can you see it fly high?
Kate's balloon, yellow and gay,
Bounced on the road far away.
Dane's balloon small and green,
Has the funniest face ever seen.
Sandy's balloon red and bright,
Has magic stars that shine at night.
Mike's balloon went hop-hop-hop
On a prickly cactus and burst POP!

Lima, the Dog

Read the poem.

Lima is a dog
Who wanted to change his spots.
So he bought a tin of white paint
To cover all the dots.

But no one seems to know him,
So he sits and waits for the rain,
Just hoping that a heavy shower
Will bring his spots again.

Put a tick (✓) on the correct option.

1. Who is Lima?

   a dog ☐ a leopard ☐

2. What did Lima want to hide?

   his tail ☐ his spots ☐

3. What does Lima wait for?

   snow ☐ rain ☐

4. Which other name would you like to give the poem?

   Lima's Spots ☐ White Paint ☐

What are We?

Can you find the missing words in this riddle poem? Give it a try! *

Please pick me up and take a look.

I have many pages. I am a

....

Hit me hard against the wall;

I will bounce back at you. I am a

....

Sit on me and have fun to float;

Sail across the water! I am a

....

I have four wheels and travel far;

I am pretty fast. I am a

....

I roll every time. Oh, it's so nice;

With numbers on me, I am a

....

*Hint: All the missing words rhyme with the word in the previous lines!

Twist your tongue

Mr. Sue's shop sells shoes for sheep.

Bubbles, Bubbles

Read the rhyme.

Bubbles, bubbles in the bath,
Seven rising here and there;
How many bubbles have to pop
To leave SIX in the air?

Six big bubbles float
And come down on the floor;
How many bubbles popped
To leave you only FOUR!

Circle the right answer.

1. What is in the bath?

   soap bubbles water

2. How many bubbles rose here and there?

   six eight seven

3. Where do six bubbles fall?

   in the tub on the floor on the head

4. How many bubbles popped to leave four?

   three five two

What's the Time?

Read the poem.

Sam's watch says it's six o'clock,
The kitchen's clock says eight,
Dad's watch says seven o'clock,
I will not be late.

Mom says that the kitchen is one hour fast
And one is one hour slow.
Dad's watch is the right one
This is all I know!

Which of these sentences is right? Put a tick (✓).

1. The poem talks about Sam's clock. ☐
2. The kitchen clock shows six o'clock. ☐
3. Sam's watch is one hour slow. ☐
4. Only one watch shows the right time. ☐
5. Dad's watch shows eight o'clock. ☐

Can you guess whose watch is one hour slow?

The Odd One

Read the text.

Susie's socks were all pretty I say.
But they fell out of her drawer one day.
Susie is puzzled. She looks here and there
to match the scattered pairs.
Can you help her sort and find the odd
one lying there?

Circle the correct answer.

1. How were Susie's socks?

   old pretty torn

2. Where does Susie keep her socks?

   in the cupboard in the basket in the drawer

3. What is another word for puzzled?

   sad happy confused

Which one is the odd one?

Plink Plonk Fun

Read the story.

The cats had a party in Granny's house

They played piano tunes

Plink plonk plank plinkle....

And made the white and black keys tinkle.

"You will never be as good on the piano as I am", laughed Granny as she played more plinkles and plonkles.

It sounded so nice that the cats went fast asleep under the stars that twinkle.

Tick (✓) the correct answer.

1. Which one is a piano?

 ☐  ☐ ☐

2. What is another good title for the story?

Cat Party ☐ Piano tunes ☐ Plinkle and Plonkle ☐

3 What did the cats do when Granny played piano?

fell asleep ☐ danced ☐ ran away ☐

Fill in the missing word.

Stars twinkle but the sun ____________.

Biscuits for Tea

Read the text.

Four children Maria, Mary, Martin and me were having tea.
We all like having biscuits with tea. Martin is greedy.
He gobbles eight biscuits. Mary takes only two.
I take only one and Maria eats four.
There are no biscuits left now.
Can you count carefully and find how
many biscuits were there altogether?

Tick (✓) the correct answer.

1. How many children were having tea?

   five ☐ three ☐ four ☐

2. Who ate eight biscuits?

   Maria ☐ Martin ☐ Mary ☐

3. How many biscuits were left?

   zero ☐ one ☐ two ☐

Take a Break!

Draw a line to fit these biscuits in the tray.

What was the total number of biscuits at tea?

____

Ronny's Bicycle

Read the story.

Ronny has a bicycle. The bicycle has wheels, a handle, and carrier just like other bicycles. It also has a bell on the handle but doesn't have a lock. It has pedals. Ronny took his bicycle for a race with his friends. His friend Kip won the race.

Write R for things that Ronny's bicycle has. Write D for things that are different.

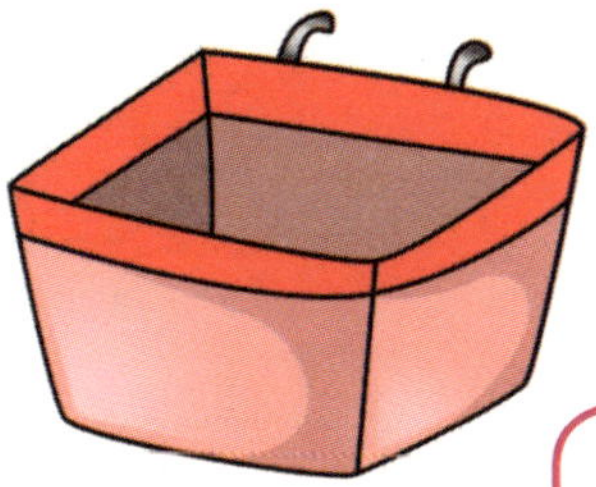

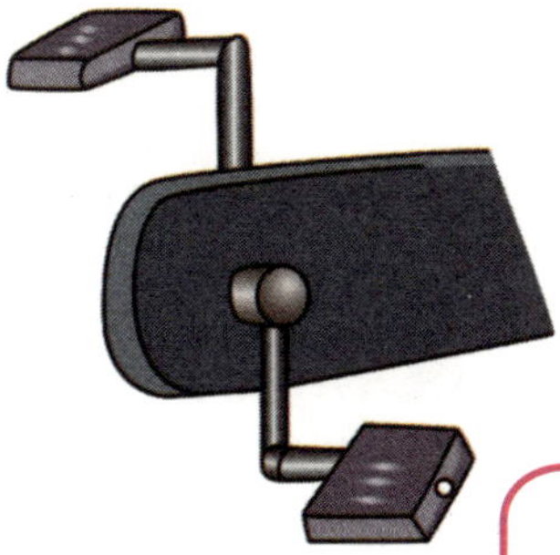

What does Ronny's bicycle have on the handle?

The Lost Goggles

Read the story.

Fred was sad. He lost his brown goggles. He looked everywhere for it- under the bed, behind the chair, in the cupboard but couldn't find it. He went to the garden and asked Ginger, the cat. "Do you know where my goggles are?" "Miaooow, No...ask the bird" said Ginger. So Fred ran to the bird. "Birdie, have you seen my goggles?" asked Fred. Birdie found it and said, "They are on your head!" You put it there and just forgot!" Fred laughed and said, "Oh! How silly I am!"

Tick (✓) the correct answers.

1. Which one are goggles?

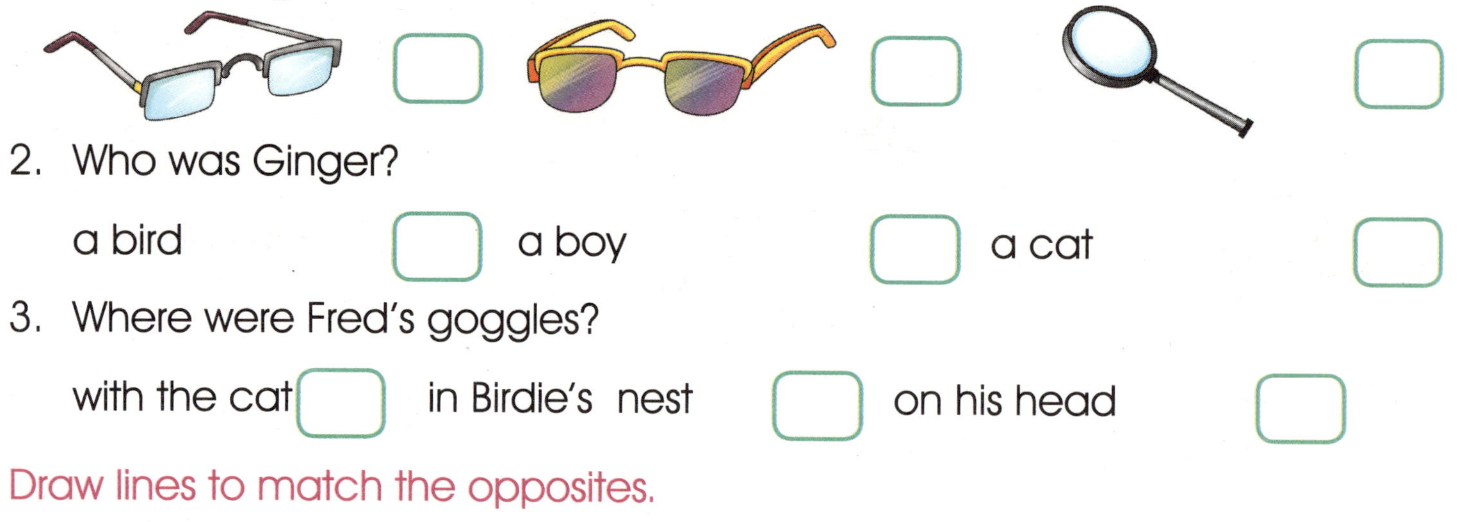

2. Who was Ginger?

a bird ☐ a boy ☐ a cat ☐

3. Where were Fred's goggles?

with the cat ☐ in Birdie's nest ☐ on his head ☐

Draw lines to match the opposites.

sad	found
lost	happy

Big Hat

Read the story.

Everyone called Sam – Big Hat. But why?

In winter he wore a woolen cap.

It covered his head. It came down to his shoulders too.

And it kept him very warm.

In summer, he wore a great cowboy hat.

It was wider than him. Sam had to bend sideways to get through the front door!

Fill in the blanks with words from the story.

1. Everyone called Sam ____________.
2. He wore a ____________ in winter.
3. Sam's summer hat was ____________ than him.
4. His woolen hat came down to his ____________.

Can you guess why Sam was called Big Hat? Write it here.

____

Answer Key

Page 2

Page 3

1. Uncle Choco Pops
2. $2.00
3. Tip and Sip Bowl
4. 200 gms

Page 4

1. dog show (fish show) car show
2. Just 15 June 10 (June 12)
3. $2 $5 ($0)
4. (10:00 am–5:00 pm) 9:00 am–6:00 pm

   6:00 pm–9:00pm

Page 5

1. (Alice) Melissa Jack
2. four years three years (five years)
3. (January 19) March 19 June 15
4. Farmland Joy Circus (Hotel Blossoms)

Page 6

1. You should stand on zoo fences. ☐
2. You can feed the animals. ☐
3. Climb over the fence and lean to see the animals. ☐

4. Animals may fall sick by eating your food. ✓

5. Do not tease animals. ✓

Page 7

Page 8

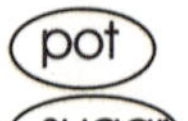

(jars)	(boy)	bag	(pot)
(stirrer)	stool	milk can	(sugar)
(mouse)	(spoon)	(napkins)	(bowl)

Page 9

Children will do on their own.

Page 10

Children will do on their own.

Make a guess answer: needle

Page 11

1. Little Duck and Mama Duck walk along the road.

2. They are going to the pond.

3. Little Duck and Mama Duck sit by the pond.

4. Mama Duck teaches Little Duck to swim.

5. Little Duck swims by herself now.

Page 12

1.  

2. 

3.  

4. 

Page 13

1. 

2. 

3. 

4. 

5.

Page 14

1. 

2. 

3. 

4. 

5. 

Page 15

To eat	To play with	To ride on
candy floss	teddy bear	merry go round
ice cream	ball	swings
pizza	doll	

Page 16

1. 

2. 

3. 

4. 

Page 17

Page 18

1. pot
2. seed
3. soil
4. water
5. sun
6. plant

Page 19

Pink: John

Yellow: Kate

Green: Dane

Red: Sandy

Blue: Mike

Page 20

1. Who is Lima?

   a dog ✓ a leopard ☐

2. What did Lima want to hide?

   his tail ☐ his spots ✓

3. What does Lima wait for?

   snow ☐ rain 

4. Children will do on their own.

Page 21

book

ball

boat

car

dice

Page 22

What is in the bath?

soap (bubbles) water

How many bubbles rose here and there?

six eight (seven)

Where do six bubbles fall?

in the tub (on the floor) on the head

How many bubbles popped to leave four?

three five (two)

Page 23

1. The poem talks about Sam's clock. ☐
2. The kitchen clock shows six o'clock. ☐
3. Sam's watch is one hour slow. ☑
4. Only one watch shows the right time. ☑
5. Dad's watch shows eight o'clock. ☐

Sam's watch is one hour slow.

Page 24

1. How were Susie's socks?
   old | (pretty) | torn
2. Where does Susie keep her socks?
   in the cupboard | in the basket | (in the drawer)
3. What is another word for puzzled?
   sad | happy | (confused)

Page 25

1. Which one is a piano?   
   ☐ ☑ ☐
2. What is another good title for the story?
   Cat Party ☐ Piano tunes ☐ Plinkle and Plonkle ☑
3. What did the cats do when Granny played piano?
   fell asleep ☑ danced ☐ ran away ☐

Page 26

1. How many children were having tea?
   five ☐ three ☐ four ☑
2. Who ate eight biscuits?
   Maria ☐ Martin ☑ Mary ☐
3. How many biscuits were left?
   zero ☑ one ☐ two ☐

There were fifteen biscuits.

Page 27

R D
R R D 

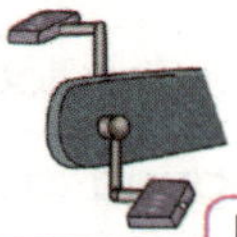

Ronnie's bicycle has a bell on the handle.

Page 28

1. Which one are goggles?   
   ☐ ☑ ☐
2. Who was Ginger?
   a bird ☐ a boy ☐ a cat ☑
3. Where were Fred's goggles?
   with the cat ☐ in Birdie's nest ☐ on his head ☑

Page 29

1. Big Hat
2. woollen cap
3. wider
4. shoulders

Because he wore a big cowboy hat.